Tattoos and Secret Societies

Jason Porterfield

ROSEN
PUBLISHING®

New York

Published in 2009 by The Rosen Publishing Group, Inc.
29 East 21st Street, New York, NY 10010

First Edition

Library of Congress Cataloging-in-Publication Data

Porterfield, Jason.
Tattoos and secret societies / Jason Porterfield.—1st ed.
    p. cm**.**—(Tattooing)
Includes bibliographical references.
ISBN-13: 978-1-4042-1827-7 (library binding)
1. Tattooing. 2. Gangs. 3. Secret societies. I. Title.
GT2345.P67 2008
 391.6'5—dc22

                                                         200704864

Manufactured in Malaysia

On the cover: Members of the Pico Norte 19th Street gang flashing their tattoos in El Paso, Texas.

Contents

INTRODUCTION

Secret societies are organizations that hide some or all of their activities from the public. They are usually closely knit, with members who depend on each other for making sure that the organization operates smoothly. They almost always have a clear chain of command, a set of rules that must be obeyed, and punishments for members who break the rules.

Many secret societies are criminal organizations. Their activities break the law, forcing them to keep their organizations closed to the public. They may be street gangs, prisoners, or global organized crime outfits. Other secret societies, such as Masonic orders and college fraternities, may be completely harmless, yet they develop a shadowy reputation because of their secrecy.

Secret societies often develop ways for their members to communicate with each other without letting others know what they're saying. They may use hand signals, code words, or even drawings and clothing to pass along a message or let other members know who they are. Usually, other members of the public won't know what these signals mean or even recognize them as a means of communication. Keeping this knowledge a secret is particularly important if the people who share it are in prison or near the territory of a rival.

An officer of the Los Angeles Police Department checks the tattoos of an 18th Street gang member just after making an arrest. Gang tattoos can often help police officers identify suspects and link them to earlier crimes.

Tattoos are another way in which secret society members communicate. A tattoo design can speak volumes about the person wearing it, announcing who the person is affiliated with, where the person is from, and the person's rank. For members of criminal organizations, the tattoo may announce their criminal specialty, whether they've killed someone, or whether they've been in prison. Tattoos forever link the person to the organization. Once a secret society member gets a tattoo, the member will have a constant, permanent reminder of his or her involvement in a secret society.

CHAPTER 1

A Look at Tattooing

In 1991, a pair of hikers traveling through the Austrian Alps came across a body partially frozen in ice. The body turned out to be the mummified remains of a man—nicknamed "Otzi" for the region in which he was found—who had died more than 5,300 years ago. Well preserved by the ice, Otzi's remains and the tools he carried have taught researchers a great deal about the time period in which he lived. Among other discoveries, scientists found that Otzi had several tattoos on his left wrist, along his spine, and on his legs and feet. The fact that the markings could still be seen testifies to the permanence of one of the world's oldest art forms.

Tattoos are permanent designs made by inserting ink below the skin. They can be simple or elaborate works of art. They may cover large areas of the body or take up very little space. Some tattoos feature colored inks, while many others are done in green or black. A tattoo's quality often depends on a tattoo artist's skills and his or her ability to draw the design that a person chooses.

Ancient Art

Otzi's tattoos are among the oldest ever found. However, evidence suggests that tattooing dates back to an even earlier period. Tattooing instruments, such as bone needles and clay ink pots, have been found at archaeological sites throughout Europe, some at least ten thousand years old. Many tattooed mummies have been recovered from ancient Egyptian sites, as well as other parts of Africa. Tattooed mummies found in South America, Asia, and the Pacific Islands show that tattooing was a widespread practice in many different cultures.

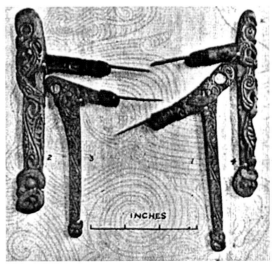

The Maoris of New Zealand created tattoos using chisels made of bone, shark's teeth, stone, or wood, which were struck by mallets to cut deep into skin.

Ancient peoples wore tattoos for many reasons. Their tattoos may have had religious significance, linking them to a god or goddess whose favor they sought or to spirits whose strength they wished to summon. Warriors may have covered their bodies in tattoos to frighten their enemies. Some ancient cultures likely viewed tattooing as a form of therapy as well. For example, some of Otzi's tattoos were found on his knee and his ankles, where the joints show evidence of wear caused by arthritis.

Tattoos also served as a way to distinguish one particular group from the rest of society. Warriors in cultures ranging from

The upper-status members of Maori society often tattooed their faces, much like this chief's son, in a drawing from sometime between 1768 and 1771. As they aged, they would add more decoration to the designs.

the British Isles to the Polynesian islands of Tonga and Samoa proudly displayed their status by wearing elaborate tattoos. In many cases, the people who applied tattoos were highly regarded priests who had trained for years before being allowed to tattoo others. As a contrast, ancient Greeks and Romans tattooed crude marks on criminals and slaves as a way to identify them.

Tattoos eventually fell out of favor throughout much of Europe and were largely forbidden by religious authorities for several centuries. At the same time, tattooing continued to thrive among Asian, Native American, and Polynesian cultures. Many European explorers, soldiers, and sailors who traveled to distant countries would return home with exotic designs on their bodies, tattoos that came to be associated with defiance and rebellion.

British explorer Captain James Cook, famous for his voyages to the Pacific Islands, played a major role in reintroducing tattooing to Europe during the 1770s. Cook's crew members would return to their ports with stories about the distant islands of New Zealand, Tahiti, or Hawaii, as well as tattoos done in the style of the Pacific Island cultures. Cook's crews, along with other explorers, would also bring back heavily tattooed islanders, who were often put on display so that the public could see their many tattoos. European performers and entertainers soon began covering their own bodies in tattoos as a way to attract public attention and make money.

Tattooing also became popular with people who wanted to distinguish themselves from mainstream society. Though some successful individuals were tattooed, many people associated the practice with sailors and criminals who frequented the rough-and-tumble waterfronts of European port cities. Instead of the marks of strength and beauty that they once were, tattoos were instead looked upon negatively by society. This was especially true in the United States and Great Britain in the nineteenth century. In the United States, released convicts were often tattooed, as were deserters from the British army. In later years, prisoners in Nazi concentration camps were marked with tattoos.

Today, tattoos aren't seen in the same negative light. There are currently several magazines for tattoo enthusiasts, often profiling artists or design types. Dozens of tattoo conventions, where artists and tattoo enthusiasts get together to show off their tattoos, take place around the United States every year. Many people from all walks of life are tattooed, including doctors, actors, teachers, musicians, and even politicians. The designs that they choose may come from any number of different cultures, or they may be an animal or portrait with which a person identifies. Most often, the tattoo is meant as a permanent expression of who a person is and how the person views himself or herself.

Symbols of Unity

Tattoos can also serve as symbols of unity, particularly among groups that may have shared the same experiences or hold the same beliefs. In this sense, tattoos can be a way for people to

A New York City Fire Department lieutenant displays the tattoo he got to memorialize the victims of the September 11, 2001, terrorist attacks. In the background are photographs of other firefighters who received the same tattoo.

The Tattoo Machine

Though the technology has changed, tattoos are still made in much the same way as they were in Otzi's lifetime. Tattoos are created by inserting dyes and inks below the surface of the skin. Hundreds or thousands of tiny holes are made in the skin, and the coloring agent is rubbed or injected into it. For thousands of years, these holes were all made individually with a needle or some similar sharp object.

The process of creating a tattoo today commonly involves a specially made tattoo machine that pricks the skin with several needles at once while applying coloring to create a permanent mark. Today's tattoo machines—when used by skilled professionals—can make hundreds of pinpricks per minute, a contrast to the time-consuming tattooing methods of previous centuries. The first tattoo machine was patented in 1891, making tattoos cheaper, faster, and less painful. The invention even led to a brief tattoo fad at the beginning of the twentieth century, when many middle- and upper-class people in the United States got tattoos.

Tattoo machines haven't changed much over the years. This modern machine has the same basic functions of those from centuries past.

bond. Members of a military unit may choose a particular image to symbolize their service together, or a group of friends might get matching tattoos to represent the good times that they've shared. Unless the tattoo is removed—an expensive and painful process—the person will have it as a constant reminder of his or her friends with the same tattoo.

Shared tattoos are particularly common among people with dangerous jobs, more so if their lives often depend on each other. Military personnel, police officers, and firefighters sometimes get tattoos to represent the work that they do and the people with whom they share their risky jobs. In other cases, people who share the same interests—such as members of a sports team or a club—may get tattooed together in order to represent that part of their lives. People may even be expected to get tattoos, especially if they belong to a club or organization in which most members are tattooed.

Permanent Identifiers

While tattoos have largely entered mainstream society, they are still used as identifiers by members of many underground groups and criminal organizations. In these cases, the tattoos advertise that a person belongs to a particular group. They may help group members identify each other or serve as part of an initiation rite. Once a recently accepted member of an exclusive group receives a permanent mark like a tattoo, it becomes very difficult for him or her to casually drop out.

Using tattoos to build loyalty and identify members is a very old tactic employed by gangs, criminal organizations, and other secret societies. Groups that engage in illegal activity or that have customs that outsiders might not understand need to be assured that their members will stay loyal.

Secret societies can include groups ranging from criminal organizations to fraternities and sororities. The groups may be secret because they would otherwise be punished or persecuted by other members of society. Or their secrecy may be due to illegal activities, as is the case with street gangs and organized crime syndicates.

CHAPTER 2

Street Gang Tattoos

Street gangs have been prominent in United States cities since the nineteenth century, when urban populations grew rapidly. This was particularly true in eastern cities such as New York, Boston, and Philadelphia, where many of the new city dwellers were immigrants from other countries. Many of the so-called native-born Americans—often young men with little to do—resented the new immigrants and would sometimes band together in gangs to attack them. In turn, immigrant groups formed gangs—also largely made up of unemployed young men—in order to protect themselves and their families from these attacks.

The early immigrant gangs were often sharply divided from each other by race, language, and nationality. They were proud of the cultures they came from and worked to maintain that identity by holding on to their language and national symbols. They remained in close contact with other immigrants from the same country. They also held onto old feuds and prejudices—particularly against immigrants from other nations. Immigrants from particular countries tended to live close to each other, and the street gangs "protected" these communities against rival gangs, often extorting money from shopkeepers and homeowners.

Bloody street battles often erupted as gangs tried to defend and expand their territory. Gang members had to be able to identify each other during a fight, to avoid accidentally hurting an ally. Gangs often identified themselves by the clothing that they wore, either a particular style or color combination, tactics still used by street gangs today.

The racial differences that divided street gangs during the nineteenth and early twentieth centuries are no longer as distinct as they once were, though there are often racial divisions between African American, white, and Hispanic gangs. Another major change that came about in the early twentieth century was the use of tattoos as identifying marks by gang members.

Gang tattoos can be large and elaborate or small and crude. Some may simply give the street gang's initials. Others may include any number of gang symbols, ranging from guns and skulls to dogs and drugs. Street gang tattoos may use a gang's particular symbols to signify how long a person has been a gang member, to indicate whether or not he or she has been to prison, and to show the person's standing within the gang.

Crips and Bloods

Two of the most infamous street gangs of recent decades are the Crips and the Bloods. Both gangs emerged out of South

Central Los Angeles in the late 1960s. In the early days, their memberships were almost exclusively African American, though that has changed to some extent, as other street gangs have taken up the names to intimidate their enemies. Crips use blue as their gang color, while Bloods wear red.

Both gangs expanded rapidly, with new subgroups breaking off from the parent groups and forming gang sets across the country. They also became bitter enemies, leading to many bloody gun battles as the gangs competed for territory, particularly after both

This member of the Los Angeles– based Grape Street Crips shows off a tattoo reading "Tha Hood Die Young." Statements glorifying a violent lifestyle are common among street gang members.

gangs became involved in selling crack cocaine.

Most Crip and Blood tattoos are pretty simple and are worn on the upper arm, back, or chest. They offer a clue to what part of the particular gang a member belongs to. The letters "GBC," for example, stand for the Garden Block Crips, a Crips organization based in Sacramento, while the letters "BTD" stand for a Reno, Nevada, gang called the Bite the Dust Crips. On the other hand, the letters "UBN" stand for United Blood Nation, a nationwide organization of Bloods.

Street gangs often use area codes and street numbers to identify each other. The "213" tattoo shown here represents an area code for Los Angeles.

Symbols and numbers found within Crip and Blood tattoos will represent a particular gang set, street, or neighborhood the gang controls. An example would be the Rollin' 60s Crips, who use the letters "RSC" and the number "60", sometimes illustrated with a pair of dice. Popular designs use area codes—such as the Los Angeles "213" number—and common neighborhood nicknames. In Blood terms, Los Angeles's Compton neighborhood is called "fruit town," while the Crips have nicknamed Pomona, California, "sin town."

Images of guns and common gangster terminology are often part of larger images. Different gang sets may use variations on the gang phrases "thug life" or "hard times," which refer to the gang members' devotion to their gang and their criminal lives on the street.

The People Nation

Two thousand miles away from the feuding Crips and Bloods, two large Chicago-based street gang organizations also began forming during the 1960s. The long-running war between what became the Folks Nation and the People Nation began with two African American gangs: the Disciples and the Blackstone Rangers.

At one time, the Blackstone Rangers had about six thousand members. Later, gang leader Jeff Fort split it into twenty-one separate gangs. He managed it as the Black P. Stone Nation and later as the El Rukns. Both of these gangs are grouped together as the People.

Gangs that are part of the People Nation include the Cobra Stones, the Puerto Rican Cobras, the Vice Lords, and the Latin Kings. Many of the gangs making up the People Nation have complex codes of behavior, as well as identifying colors, code words, and hand signals that enable them to communicate silently when in public.

Jeff Fort was Muslim and used Egyptian symbols like pyramids—as well as corrupted Muslim religious symbols such as a crescent moon and a five-pointed star—as his gang signifiers.

Jeff Fort of the Blackstone Rangers testifies before a Senate subcommittee in 1968. His jacket displays his gang's trademark pyramid.

These images show up in many tattoos of People Nation gang members. Tattoos may also include Chicago's "312" area code and numbers that refer to specific streets. Many feature dollar signs, dice, and martini glasses to represent the riches the gang has accumulated through its criminal activities.

The Latin Kings use many of these symbols in their tattoos, as well as five-pointed crowns and the letters "LK." They also use upside-down pitchforks to symbolize disrespect for their archenemies, a part of the Folks Nation called the Black Gangster Disciples.

The Folks Nation

The gangs linked together in the Folks Nation see all gangs linked to the People Nation as their enemies. The Folks Nation grew out of a gang called the Disciples, rivals of the old Blackstone Rangers during the 1960s. The Folks Nation now incorporates more than twenty separate gangs. Gangs that are part of the Folks Nation include the C-Notes, the Insane Popes, the Latin Jivers, the Spanish Cobras, the Satan Disciples, and the Black Gangster Disciples.

Gang Identifiers

Besides tattoos, street gangs have several ways of showing their affiliation and marking their territory. Gangs usually have an identifying color that they wear and will sometimes attack people wearing the colors of a rival gang, even non-gang members. Graffiti signs—often crudely done in spray paint—mark an area as a particular gang's territory. The sign will use some symbol or shorthand for the gang's name, such as a number or initials. Gang members might individually mark the sign with their street names, showing that they aren't afraid to identify with their gang.

Hand signs, while used to pass messages, can also be used by gang members to identify each other. When two members meet, one gang member may flash a sign, expecting the other to flash the appropriate sign in response.

The Folks Nation gangs use the six-pointed Star of David to commemorate a former Black Gangster Disciples leader named David "King David" Barksdale. This star appears frequently in Folks Nation tattoos. The number "6" is a common element, also appearing in six-pointed crowns or as two crossed three-pronged pitchforks.

The largest of the criminal gangs of the Folks Nation are the Black Gangster Disciples. The Disciples claim some thirty thousand members among their many groups, a tightly organized union ruled by a chairman and two boards of directors—one to oversee criminal operations on the streets and the other to control moneymaking crimes in prisons. Below them are fifteen regional governors who coordinate criminal activities in specific regions of the country. Winged hearts, often incorporating pitchforks and upside-down "5"s and "L"s to represent disrespect for the Latin Kings, are tattoos that are specific to the Black Gangster Disciples.

Mara Salvatrucha

Mara Salvatrucha is a street gang that emerged in El Salvador during that country's bloody civil war. By the time the war ended in 1992, more than one million Salvadoran refugees had come to the United States, settling mainly in California. Most left El Salvador to escape the violence, but some fighters left to avoid prosecution for their roles in the war. Many of these fighters came together to start the Mara Salvatrucha, or MS, which means "beware the Salvadorans." The MS began a series of brutal gang wars with other California gangs, some of which continue today as the groups fight over territory.

Mara Salvatrucha membership has expanded rapidly. The gang has established a presence in fourteen states, as well as Washington, D.C.; Canada; and several Latin American countries. There are an estimated thirty-six thousand MS members worldwide, as the gang has opened up membership to allow other South and Central Americans to join. The gang's activities include drug and weapons smuggling, kidnapping, arson, and murder for hire.

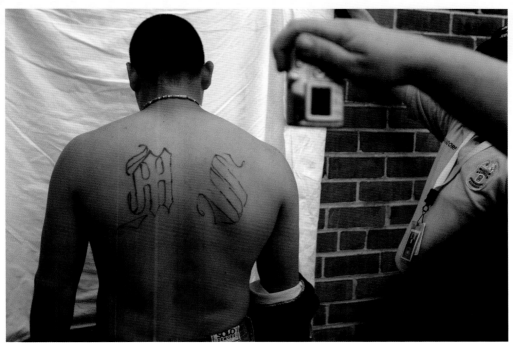

Police from the antigang unit in Prince George's County, Maryland, photograph the identifying tattoos of a suspected member of the Mara Salvatrucha for their police database.

The Salvatruchas use the number "13" as their primary symbol. Tattoos for this group often consist of the letters "MS" and some variation on the number, such as Roman numerals. The phrases "Salvadoran Pride" or "Mara with a Shotgun" are also common. Gang members usually sport many smaller tattoos as well. Daggers, dice, and crossbones frequently appear all over the body.

CHAPTER 3

Tattoos and Prison Gangs

In prisons, it's not uncommon for inmates who share a common criminal background to band together, particularly if they have been members of the same street gang or criminal organization. They create prison gangs, using their organization to intimidate non-gang members and control criminal activity within their prisons, such as dealing in drugs or weapons that have been smuggled inside.

Being part of a prison gang likely won't make most prisoners rich, but they may enjoy a certain degree of privilege and respect that they wouldn't ordinarily receive from other prisoners. This privilege and respect is based on fear, particularly fear of retaliation. When a non-gang member harms or shows disrespect to a gang member, the gang member can count on other members within the prison population for backup. Most prison gangs form along racial lines that limit membership to a specific race. They may specifically choose prisoners of another race as the targets for their abuse.

Prison tattoos often show images that represent the difficulty of serving long sentences. This prisoner's tattoo shows a blindfolded "Lady of Justice" deciding someone's fate.

Prison gangs rely on loyalty, silence, and intimidation for their existence. They have complex rules about what a prisoner may do, who he or she may talk to, and how gang members respond to commands from gang leaders. Secret signs and hand signals are vital to communicating within the controlled environment of a prison. The code of silence among prison gang members is absolutely necessary because forming gangs inside prisons is illegal. Prisoners can be punished by prison officials if the guards find out that they are taking part in gang

The designs on this inmate's back were done by prison tattoo artists. Images of Jesus, Aztec warriors, eagles, and children are common among Mexican prisoners.

activities. The punishment for breaking the code of silence is severe and could even result in death.

The Prison Tattoo

Prison tattoo artists are forced to be creative when it comes to finding equipment and materials for ink, materials that most prisons prohibit. In fact, tattooing is banned in many jails and prisons because of the risk of prisoners becoming infected or catching contagious diseases through dirty equipment. Prisoners have to make their own tattoo equipment and inks from whatever items they can get and spend many hours working in secret to avoid getting caught. If they are detected, both the tattoo artist and the prisoner receiving the tattoo are disciplined. In addition to losing privileges, the tattoo artist will likely lose the equipment and ink.

Still, prisoners find ways to get around the ban. Their crude, battery-powered tattoo guns are often fashioned from random items such as ballpoint pens, toothbrush handles, rigid bits of wire, and motors from portable cassette players. They smuggle ink from their hobby classes or make it out of soot.

When it's time to do the outline for the tattoo, they get another inmate to watch for guards, stopping if a guard starts approaching. Once the outline is done, the shading and detail work is done in a series of sessions so that the skin can heal. Under these circumstances, some tattoos can take months to complete. Though prison tattoos have long been considered one of the most crude forms of tattooing, some artists are skilled enough to use their makeshift equipment to do work that can match many conventional tattoo studios.

Racial tensions often run high among inmate populations, as some prisoners belonging to one race band together in gangs to protect themselves against threats—real or imagined—from prisoners of other races. They may develop prejudices that they never held before they went to prison. These attitudes date back to the 1960s, when race wars broke out in prisons across the United States as a reflection of the civil rights struggle going on in the rest of the country. White, African American, and Hispanic prison gangs rarely let members of other races join, and they often carry grudges against each other that erupt in violence. They wear their tattoos as a statement of their solidarity with their fellow gang members and to intimidate other prisoners.

The Aryan Brotherhood

The Aryan Brotherhood—an all-white gang—is one of the most feared prison gangs in the country. It emerged during the 1960s from the remnants of an older gang called the Blue Birds, which had used tattoos of bluebirds in flight to represent their desire for freedom. From the start, the Aryan Brotherhood modeled itself after the Nazi Party of Adolf Hitler, believing all races to be inferior to their own. They recruit only the strongest and most violent white inmates.

In the early days, anyone who wanted to become a member first had to kill someone targeted by the gang's leadership, and death was seen as the only way out of the Aryan Brotherhood. They called this initiation and lifestyle "blood in, blood out." Murder is no longer required for a prisoner to become a member, but he must still complete a mission, such as beating another prisoner or acquiring contraband items. Once the prisoner has done this—called "earning his bones"—he learns about the gang's social structure and how to abide by the Aryan Brotherhood's rules. These specify that gang members must

A Delaware prisoner on death row displays a tattoo marking him as a member of the Aryan Brotherhood. The gang's "blood in, blood out" rule prevents members from leaving.

treat other members with the utmost respect in front of non-members, always obey commands, and help each other out at all times.

As an initiation, the new member receives a tattoo of what has become the official brand of the Aryan Brotherhood —a shamrock with the number "666" as part of the design. The shamrock supposedly represents a founding member, who was Irish. The "666" is associated with Satanism and stands for the group's hatred of authority.

The Aryan Brotherhood also uses the Nazi swastika to represent its admiration for Hitler and Nazi Germany. Other common designs used by the Aryan Brotherhood include many

Soviet Prison Tattoos

From the mid-1960s to the late 1980s, the Soviet Union, which broke apart in 1991, imprisoned as many as thirty-five million people in prison camps. Of that number, between twenty million and thirty million received tattoos while serving their sentences.

The tattoos had specific meanings that were known to all inmates at a particular prison. Many were status marks that boasted of the wearer's crimes. Inmates caught wearing a tattoo that they hadn't earned or didn't deserve might be punished by death.

A murderer may have had skull tattoos, one for each victim. A single cat meant the wearer was a thief. Multiple cats indicated that the thief was part of a gang. A circle of barbed wire around the top of a prisoner's head meant he was serving a life sentence without a chance for parole.

Other tattoo designs were forced onto inmates. A skull and crossbones tattoo meant that someone had marked the prisoner for death. A playing card with a diamond indicated that the prisoner collaborated with guards. Tattoos that prisoners hadn't earned were often forcibly obscured with other designs.

symbols representing northern European history and culture, such as Viking helmets and eagles. The letters "AB" are also common, sometimes disguised within larger designs. Despite their belief in their own superiority, Aryan Brotherhood members are often attacked by other prisoners simply for wearing their identifying tattoos.

The Black Guerrilla Family

African American prison gangs were small and poorly organized until the 1960s, when the era's social changes led to the founding of well-organized radical organizations on the outside. These groups demanded social changes and equal rights for all Americans, as well as reform within prison systems that they viewed as racist. Some prisoners began picking up on these ideas and became active in trying to change the system from within. Others had different motives and used radical ideas to attract fellow prisoners to their gangs.

The Black Guerrilla Family (BGF) is one such gang. At its founding in 1966, the gang's leaders seemed to support violent efforts to overthrow the United States government. Only African American prisoners were allowed to join and take part in what leaders advertised as the coming social revolution. Many followers believed in the Communist principles of shared property and governing by a collective. The gang developed a complex chain of command and a rigid set of rules to enforce discipline. Punishments for breaking rules ranged from fines or loss of privileges to death. Many Black Guerrilla Family members also learned Swahili—an African language—in order to communicate secretly. The BGF is a longstanding enemy of the Aryan Brotherhood. Members see themselves as part of a large revolutionary struggle and consider themselves prisoners of war.

Black Guerrilla Family tattoos often use symbols that relate to the group's roots in Communism, or the belief in a society in which the government owns everything and distributes it equally to the people. A dragon wrapped around a prison tower is a common image. The dragon represents the revolutionary beliefs of the late Chinese Communist dictator Mao Tse-tung. A crossed rifle and machete stand for the bloody revolution to come. Members also use the number "276," the numerical order of the letters "BGF."

The Kumi African Nation is a California-based subset of the Black Guerrilla Family. Sometimes called the 415, they use the number—a San Francisco area code—in their tattoo designs. The most common "415" tattoo shows a warrior rising out of the African continent, signifying people of African descent rising above slavery. Often, the warrior is armed with a machine gun and holds a banner emblazoned with the number "415." Some newer versions of this tattoo, however, show the warrior holding a book instead of a gun. The book represents the gang's rules.

Like the Black Guerrilla Family, they also use Asian dragons to represent their belief in Mao Tse-tung's Communist philosophy. Other tattoos used by the 415 include the words "Forever Forever," a phrase used in opening and closing meetings, and a bleeding heart squeezed by a bear's claws.

The Mexican Mafia

The Mexican Mafia started in California in 1957, as Mexican American prisoners banded together to protect themselves against existing prison gangs. Led by former street gang members, they created an organization based on the Sicilian

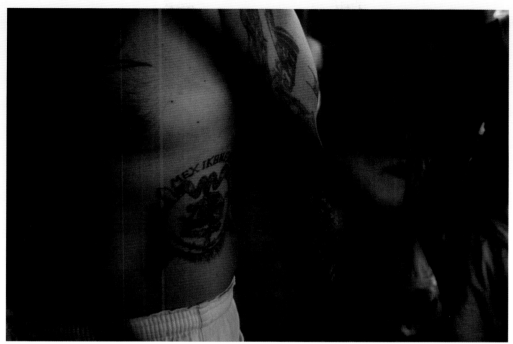

Members of the Mexican Mafia in Texas prisons often tattoo themselves with an image of an eagle and a snake to mark their heritage. The Mexican Mafia is one of the most feared prison gangs in the country.

Mafia. They even named their new gang La Mafia Mexicana, Spanish for "the Mexican Mafia." Members drew up a set of rules, including a "blood in, blood out" rule similar to that of the Aryan Brotherhood. Only Mexican Americans were allowed to join. Since its formation, the Mexican Mafia's numbers have been cut by infighting and the formation of other Mexican American prison gangs. Still, there are significant numbers of members, as well as affiliated gangs.

Mexican Mafia members are often marked with a tattoo of a black hand, with the letter "M" disguised in the creases on the palm. The letters "eMe" show up frequently, along with Mexican nationalist symbols. A common one is an eagle killing a snake, as shown on Mexico's flag. Aztec designs and symbols are also used, representing Mexico's Native American heritage and the strength and power of the old Aztec Empire.

Nuestra Familia

The Nuestra Familia is the most prominent enemy of the Mexican Mafia. The gang is based in Northern California and has fought with the Mexican Mafia—based in Southern California—for control of California prisons and smuggling territory since the late 1960s. The Nuestra Familia allows northern Hispanics to join provided that they follow the gang's code. The code specifies that members learn prison survival skills, such as how to make weapons, communicate through codes and signals, and escape from handcuffs. Mexican Mafia members are considered lifelong enemies and must be attacked on sight.

The Nuestra Familia adopted a sombrero pierced with a bloody dagger as its symbol. The image shows up frequently in the gang's tattoos. The dagger stands for the organization's rules, while the blood on its point represents gang members who have been killed in fighting. The blood that drips from the dagger is supposed to belong to the gang's enemies.

The group uses a complex tattooing system to signify a member's status as a killer. Tiny stars on a member's arm indicate that he is a "hitter," a member skilled at killing enemies. A star on the left side of the forehead indicates that a member has successfully completed a hit. Hitters are also designated by a single tear outlined below the corner of the eye. If the teardrop is filled in, it means that the hitter has successfully completed five hits. Other tattoos include the words "Nuestra Familia," the letters "NF," and the number "14."

CHAPTER 4

The Tattoos of Organized Crime

Organized crime is a sprawling worldwide business, covering hundreds of illegal activities in dozens of countries. The groups involved are very organized and hierarchical, which means that members' ranks depend upon either their skills or their connections to group leaders.

The goal of organized crime is to secure wealth and power through both legal and illegal activities. Members of these groups may be linked to each other by ethnicity or kinship, or simply by their secrets and the code of behavior that each crime group follows. They speak in codes and use secret signs and signals in order to protect themselves from the police.

Organized crime outfits tend to create monopolies on their industries, which means they intimidate competitors so they control the whole market. Often, this is done illegally, either by using threats or violence. Unlike street gangs, they often hide their crimes behind their legal businesses, using them as a cover and reinvesting their criminal profits in order to make even more money.

Organized crime outfits also differ from street gangs in the level of sophistication that they bring to their activities. Because of their wealth, they can invest a great deal of money in bribes and hiring highly skilled criminal specialists, from computer hackers to kidnappers. This wealth also gives them the ability to switch their operations from one focus to another, such as from drugs to human trafficking.

Few street gangs are as durable as organized crime outfits or have the same level of political protection. Nor do they have the same mystique as criminal organizations such as the Russian Mafiya, the Japanese Yakuza, or the Chinese Triads. Street gangs may pattern themselves after these organizations, yet they simply do not have the same global reach. Many of these groups, however, are linked to street gangs by their use of tattoos.

One exception is the Mafia, possibly the largest and most successful criminal organizations in the world. Though individual members may get tattoos, neither the Sicilian Mafia nor its affiliates in the United States have a tradition of tattooing.

The Yakuza

The Yakuza is the Japanese version of the Mafia, though the two groups are not linked to each other. The word "Yakuza" itself comes from a losing score from a Japanese card game, and many Yakuza members consider themselves to be misfits, losers, or outcasts. The Yakuza's origins are shrouded in mystery. It likely started sometime before the mid-nineteenth century,

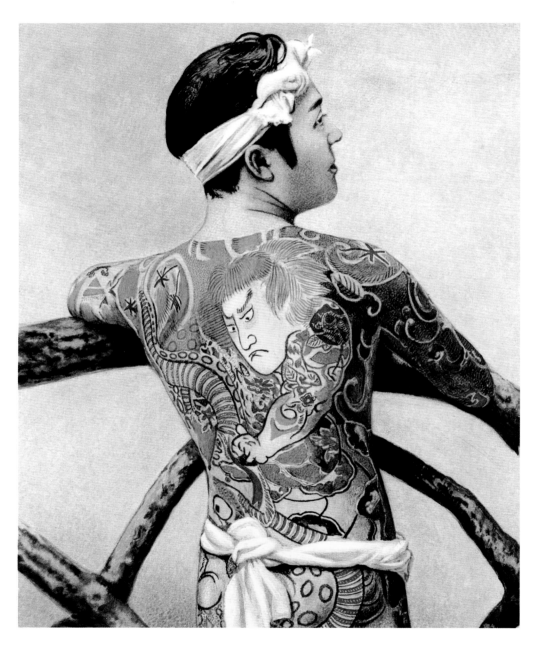

Full-body tattoo designs were once common among Yakuza members. Today, many younger Yakuza choose smaller designs to make themselves less noticeable.

when wandering bands of warriors began terrorizing villages. Yakuza members claim to be descended from the gangs of villagers that formed to fight off these warriors.

Yakuza syndicates place a great deal of importance on traditions and rituals. Members claim to be the last element of Japanese society to follow the ways of the samurai—warriors who placed honor and duty before anything else, including their own lives. They are said to believe in a moral duty to exact revenge on their enemies, as well as a need for compassion for ordinary people. Often, Yakuza activities are overlooked or ignored by the public because of these qualities and their supposed link to Japanese history.

Japanese officials, who like to project the image of a law-and-order society, often deny evidence of Yakuza activity. Yakuza crimes often include arson, blackmail, and murder. Its organizations are often linked to high-tech financial crimes and have been known to drain huge sums of money from Japanese corporations.

Traditions among the Yakuza include a willingness to accept blame when ordered to do so by gang bosses and to go to prison in order to protect the organization's interests. When a Yakuza member fails to carry out a task, he may be asked to cut off one of his finger joints in order to show that his apology is sincere. In extreme cases, members may be asked to kill themselves.

Full-body tattoos among Yakuza members are one of their oldest and most visible traditions. These tattoos are often extremely elaborate and colorful. The tradition dates to the

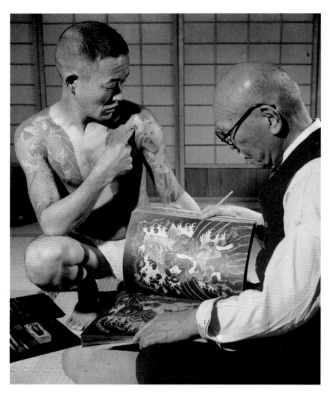

A Japanese tattoo artist helps a Yakuza gang member choose a design. Yakuza tattoos often include images from Japanese history and mythology.

seventeenth and eighteenth centuries, when such tattoos were common among warriors, firemen, and policemen. Traditional Yakuza tattoos are done only on parts of the body ordinarily covered by clothing, such as the chest or back. They depict dragons, flowers, samurai warriors in traditional dress, landscapes, abstract designs, and Japanese mythological figures. Younger Yakuza members may have modern gangland tools done in a traditional style, such as pistols or motorcycles. The neck, hands, and feet were traditionally left unmarked, though some younger Yakuza are now tattooed in those places.

The pride that Yakuza members take in following Japanese traditions leads many to reject tattoo guns when the time comes for them to get their tattoos. Instead, they have their tattoos done in a traditional way by artists using bamboo tools. This method of tattooing is a long and painful process. Some of the full-body designs may take over one hundred hours to complete, making the Yakuza tattoos a badge of the member's courage and toughness.

The Chinese Triads

Chinese Triad societies began in the seventeenth century as an effort to drive all foreigners out of China. They existed as nationalist social groups for many decades before eventually evolving into criminal organizations. The Triad societies turned to crime around the beginning of the twentieth century, when it became clear that they couldn't keep other nations from taking advantage of China's resources. Today, their criminal activities include extortion, money laundering, drug trafficking, and gambling, all of which generate billions of dollars each year.

Triad power is concentrated in the Chinese city of Hong Kong, where an estimated eighty thousand Triad members are said to operate. Like other major criminal organizations, the Triads are a global criminal network, with elements based throughout Asia, in Europe, and in North and South America.

As the Triads moved away from political and cultural interests to criminal activities, they began incorporating many secret rituals and ceremonies into their meetings and interactions. New members are carefully screened and must have a family member or close friend as a sponsor, as a way of keeping police informers out. The initiation ceremony for new members includes several traditional ceremonies that once lasted for days. One, called "the passing of the mountain of swords,"

Tattoo Removal

Though tattoos are meant to be permanent, thousands of people every year have them removed. Years ago, tattoo removal was so difficult and painful that few attempted it. A method called dermabrasion consisted of sanding the design off the skin. Cryosurgery was when the tattoo was frozen and rubbed away. Excision meant that the surgeon cut the image away with a scalpel and then closed the wound with stitches.

Today, lasers are often used to break down the tattoo pigments. Laser removal, however, can be expensive and may not even remove all of the tattoo. Certain pigments—usually green and yellow—don't break down easily, and the procedure still hurts.

requires the new member to walk calmly under swords held just above his head. Another involves beheading a live chicken and drinking a portion of its blood mixed with wine.

Oaths are important to the Triads, and members are expected to know and keep a set of thirty-six that have been passed down from the founding of these groups. They are also expected to know elaborate hand signals and code words that enable members to communicate privately when they are around nonmembers.

Though not as colorful or elaborate as Yakuza tattoos, Triad tattoos are often highly detailed works of art. They depict Chinese cultural symbols—such as dragons or tigers—as well

This Triad member has a tattoo of two dragons fighting for a pearl. The dragons symbolize two ancient dynasties, while the pearl stands for the throne of China.

as scenes from Chinese history and mythology. Warriors are frequently used, as well as legendary emperors. More discreet members may use a simple pattern of three dots arranged in the shape of a triangle. The number "3" has magical properties in many Chinese myths. After joining, new Triad members are even assigned numbers divisible by three, as well as a title and rank.

Triad tattoos often include hidden information in their design, details that another Triad member would be expected to notice and understand. Warriors or mythological figures, for example, may be depicted giving hand signs, or shapes within the designs may indicate a specific Triad gang.

The Russian Mafiya

When the Soviet Union collapsed in 1991, many of the former member nations fell into political chaos. Criminal organizations in former Soviet republics such as Russia and the Ukraine seized this opportunity and began expanding. They recruited former military personnel, police, political prisoners who had been released, and even government workers. These criminal organizations are often called the Russian Mafiya, or the Vodka Dons, for their involvement in bootlegging and smuggling vodka. Other criminal operations include telecommunications fraud, drug trafficking, weapons smuggling, and even illegally selling human organs for use in transplants. Their organizations span the world, with thousands of members in U.S. cities such as New York, Los Angeles, Chicago, Boston, and San Francisco.

Russian Mafiya leaders are often easy to spot. They may mimic the flashy style of the American gangsters of the 1920s and 1930s, wearing long overcoats and using expensive limousines to move around their cities. Members communicate through hand signals, codes, and even facial expressions.

Many members, especially those who spent time in Soviet prisons, are tattooed. The prison tattoos often represented a prisoner's rank within the prison culture, with additional tattoos showing their climb up the ranks, or their disgrace. Playing

A member of the Russian Mafiya displays his tattoos, which were acquired in a Siberian prison camp. The eight-pointed stars at the front of his shoulders indicate his status as a godfather.

card suits—aces, clubs, hearts, and diamonds—are frequently used in tattoo designs. Even after prisoners are released, their tattoos continue to represent their standing within the criminal world. Prison bosses—called Pakhans—often have eight-pointed stars tattooed on the front of their shoulders. The Pakhans usually continue to hold high rank within the Mafiya after their release.

Mafiya tattoos often indicate the degree of authority a member has within the organization. A crown shows that a member has some authority. A bird of prey with a cat's paw instead of a head may signify a senior, high-ranking Mafiya member. Another common tattoo for Mafiya leadership is a dagger with a serpent wrapped around it. The serpent often has a crown above its head. Skulls, American dollars, and American gangsters are all common tattoos among Mafiya leaders.

CHAPTER 5

Other Tattooed Secret Societies

ecret societies are found everywhere. Though many are criminal organizations, some societies are secret because members enjoy the secrecy. They may remain secret because other elements of society disapprove of what they do, even if their activities aren't necessarily illegal.

Freemasons

Masonic organizations are ancient societies. Some historians and members claim that Masonic orders date back as far as Europe's Middle Ages. They link Masons to the Knights Templar, a group that was founded during the Middle Ages to protect religious pilgrims traveling from Europe to Jerusalem. On one level, they function as trade organizations, with members often sharing a profession such as masonry or carpentry. Locally, Masonic lodges take active roles in their communities, performing volunteer work or raising money for charity through community events. At present,

Images from an 1820 French book on Freemasonry show the points of the compass and other symbols related to the Freemasons. Freemasons have long been famous for their secret symbols and rituals.

Masonic orders in the United States have an estimated 1.8 million members.

Freemasons have been viewed with suspicion because of their secrecy. Masonic lodges keep their meetings and rituals from the general public and have systems of code words and signals, as well as strict codes of behavior. They have a strict chain of command, counted by degrees. A new member is ranked at the first degree, while members with the highest ranking are considered thirty-third degree.

Conspiracy theorists believe that the Freemasons are secretly involved in running many world governments, particularly that of the United States. They use the fact that twenty-five U.S. presidents belonged to Masonic orders and the long list of other prominent Freemasons—including politicians, military leaders, and entertainers—as proof. Other criticisms link the Freemasons to witchcraft and devil worship, a charge based on their secret rituals and occasionally leveled by Christian church leaders. Critics also point out their refusals to admit women and allegations of racism, as some Masonic groups continue to maintain separate lodges for their white and African American members.

Though they are not supposed to reveal the nature of their rituals, most Masons take pride in their organization and display its signs and symbols. The most common is the square and compass—carpentry tools that represent the Freemasons' link to builders—that are crossed to form a diamond, called the Master's Jewel. Other symbols include pyramids, scimitars, Egyptian symbols, and eyes.

The Priory of Sion

Historical evidence supports the existence of a monastic order based in Jerusalem called the Priory of Sion, which served as a way station for pilgrims until it was absorbed by the Jesuit monastic order in 1617.

According to legend, the priory is also a secret society that has spent hundreds of years defending the secret heirs of Jesus Christ. Alleged members through history are said to include artist Leonardo da Vinci, scientist Isaac Newton, composer Claude Debussy, and writers Jules Verne and Victor Hugo. However, evidence strongly suggests that this aspect of the Priory of Sion was really a hoax, invented by a Catholic priest named François Bérenger Saunière and his housekeeper, Marie Denarnaud. Others later used the hoax to further their own agendas, enhancing it by including details about a vast treasure concealed in the French countryside.

Today, some people believe that the Priory of Sion exists in secret. Members supposedly use tattoos to identify each other, including variations on the fleur-de-lis, an old French symbol said to represent the lily. The recent best-selling novel *The Da Vinci Code* and the movie it inspired have helped renew interest in the story.

Members of the Priory of Sion often displayed tattoos of the fleur-de-lis to symbolize their unity.

Freemasons are not required to be tattooed, but many Masons of all ages get tattoos depicting the symbols of their order. The square and compass is a popular design for Masons, and it may be worked into larger designs or include a member's rank. Scimitars and stars are also common in Masonic tattoo designs.

Motorcycle Gangs

Motorcycle gangs first began forming in the United States shortly after the end of World War II. Many members were military veterans and social misfits who projected a rebellious attitude in the way they dressed and lived. Many had little regard for the law and became involved in crimes ranging from drug trafficking to making fake IDs. Over the years, their brawling and antiauthority lifestyles have repeatedly upset the public and made headlines. The most famous motorcycle gang is the Hell's Angels, based in San Bernadino, California. Other biker gangs have similarly fierce names, such as the Outlaws, the Pagans, and the Bandidos.

Biker gangs are closely knit groups that spend a great deal of time together, either riding their motorcycles or working on them. Despite their distaste for authority, many choose leaders, often based on toughness and street smarts. They have very few rules, most of which warn against stealing from other members or touching other people's motorcycles without permission.

Motorcycle groups often show their unity with their tattoos. They are also frequently bonded by being veterans of war. These motorcyclists are participating in the 17th annual Memorial Day Rolling Thunder Rally to commemorate those lost and missing in the Vietnam War.

Gang members are expected to get tattoos, and many are heavily tattooed with a variety of designs. Some gangs have official symbols, and members may have their gang chapter or their hometown worked into their designs. The Hell's Angels use a winged skull as their symbol, and members often have a tattoo of this design.

Motorcycles are very common design elements, as are skulls and daggers. Some motorcycle gang members are very patriotic and may have American flags or bald eagles worked into their tattoos. Others use Nazi symbols, either to scare non-members or as expressions of their racism. Still others may use religious symbols, such as crosses or portraits of Jesus Christ.

Fraternities and Sororities

Joining a fraternity or sorority is a rite of passage for many young college students. Fraternities and sororities are social networks based on college campuses across the United States. Fraternities are specifically for men, while sororities are for women only. The first fraternity in the United States formed in 1776, while the first sorority formed in 1851.

Fraternities and sororities first developed as secret societies, and membership was by invitation only. The groups identified themselves by sets of Greek letters and created secret mottos, rules, handshakes, and rituals to set themselves apart from other students. They lived together as roommates in charter houses, which became the center of their activities. Fraternities and sororities are often associated with parties and pranks, but many also do volunteer work to fulfill their organization's requirements.

Today, new members are initiated into fraternities and sororities, rather than invited. Once the new members are initiated into the group through several rituals, secret rituals and traditions may be revealed to them. Members often keep in touch with each other after college and sometimes become part of larger national networks. No fraternity or sorority requires members to get tattoos, though several members may go to an artist together as a show of friendship and solidarity. Some fraternity and sorority members feel so strongly about their membership that they get tattoos of their organization's Greek letters. The letters will forever mark them as members.

GLOSSARY

arthritis Inflammation of a joint or joints.

Communist A person who believes that all property should be shared; also describes a totalitarian system of government in which private property is eliminated and the state owns all means of production.

compass A drafting tool used for drawing circles.

conspiracy A crime committed by a group banded together in secret for some illegal or harmful purpose.

contraband Items that are illegal to own or sell.

emblazon To decorate or mark, as with a design.

exploit To use or take advantage of a person or situation for gain.

extort To obtain something through intimidation.

hierarchical Classified according to certain information, such as age or experience.

mystique A sense of something being more interesting or powerful than usual.

nationalist Devoted to the interests and culture of one particular nation.

Nazi Someone who believes in the ideas of the Nazi Party, which advocated the superiority of Germans over all other people.

prominent Obviously important or meaningful.

scimitar A type of curved sword that originated in Asia.

shamrock A type of clover with bright green, heart-shaped leaves.

Soviet Union A former Communist country in eastern Europe and northern Asia that existed from 1922 to 1991. It included Russia and fourteen other Soviet Socialist republics.

square A hand tool consisting of two straight arms at right angles, used to construct or test right angles.

stigma A symbol of disgrace.

Swahili A language widely spoken throughout east and central Africa.

swastika The official emblem of the Nazi Party; a cross with the arms bent at right angles in a clockwise direction.

syndicate A loose affiliation of gangsters in charge of organized criminal activities.

For More Information

Alliance of Professional Tattooists
A.P.T., Inc.
9210 S. Highway 17-92
Maitland, FL 32751
(407) 831-5549
Web site: http://www.safe-tattoos.com
The Alliance of Professional Tattooists is an educational organization founded
  to address health and safety issues within the tattoo industry.

**Ancient and Accepted Scottish Rite of Freemasons
of Canada**
Grand Secretary-General
Donald N Campbell, 33°
4 Queen Street South
Hamilton, ON L8P 3R3
Canada
(905) 522-0033
E-mail: supreme33@scottishritemasons-can.org
Web site: http://www.scottishritemasons-can.org
A national organization of master Freemasons based in Canada.

**The Jack and Mae Nathanson Centre on Transnational
Human Rights, Crime, and Security**
Room 409M, Osgoode Hall Law School
York University
4700 Keele Street

Toronto, ON M3J 1P3
Canada
(416) 736-5907
E-mail: orgcrime@yorku.ca
Web site: http://www.yorku.ca/nathanson/default.htm
This center has extensive databases and information on organized crime in
North America.

National Alliance of Gang Investigators' Associations
P.O. Box 608628
Orlando, FL 32860
(321) 388-8694
E-mail: RustyKeeble@fgia.com
Web site: http://www.nagia.org
This is a national organization of law enforcement personnel who specialize
in investigating street gangs.

The National Tattoo Association
485 Business Park Lane
Allentown, PA 18109
(610) 433-7261
E-mail: curt@nationaltattoo.com
Web site: http://www.nationaltattooassociation.com
The National Tattoo Association operates an annual convention that has been
running for twenty-eight years.

The Tattoo Archive
618 West 4th Street
Winston-Salem, NC 27101
(366) 722-4422

E-mail: tattoo@tattooarchive.com

Web site: http://www.tattooarchive.com

The Tattoo Archive encompasses a design museum, a research center, and a
bookstore.

Web Sites

Due to the changing nature of Internet links, Rosen Publishing
has developed an online list of Web sites related to the subject
of this book. This site is updated regularly. Please use this link
to access the list:

http://www.rosenlinks.com/ttt/tass

FOR FURTHER READING

Black, Andy. *Organized Crime*. Broomall, PA: Mason Crest Publishers, 2003.

Currie-McGhee, Leanne K. *Tattoos and Body Piercing*. Detroit, MI: Lucent Books, 2006.

Gay, Kathlyn. *Body Marks: Tattoos, Piercings*. Brookfield, CT: Twenty-First Century, 2002.

Gifford, Clive. *Gangs*. North Mankato, MN: Smart Apple Media, 2007.

Mason, Paul. *Tattoos and Body Piercings*. Portsmouth, NH: Heinemann Library, 2003.

Ross, Stewart. *Secret Societies*. London, England: Aladdin/Watts, 1996.

Stark, Evan. *Everything You Need to Know About Street Gangs*. New York, NY: Rosen Publishing, 2000.

BIBLIOGRAPHY

DeMello, Margo. *Bodies of Inscription: A Cultural History of the Modern Tattoo Community*. Durham, NC: Duke University Press, 2000.

Gilbert, Steve, ed. *Tattoo History: A Source Book*. New York, NY: Juno Books, 2000.

Green, Terisa. *Ink: The Not-Just-Skin-Deep Guide to Getting a Tattoo*. New York, NY: New American Library, 2005.

Lunde, Paul. *Organized Crime: An Insider's Guide to the World's Most Successful Industry*. New York, NY: Dorling Kindersley Limited, 2004.

Reynolds, John Lawrence. *Secret Societies: Inside the World's Most Notorious Organizations*. New York, NY: Arcade Publishing, 2006.

Steward, Samuel M. *Bad Boys and Tough Tattoos: A Social History of the Tattoo with Gangs, Sailors, and Street-Corner Punks*. New York, NY: Harrington Park Press, 1990.

Valentine, Bill. *Gang Intelligence Manual*. Boulder, CO: Paladin Press, 1995.

Valentine, Bill. *Gangs and Their Tattoos: Identifying Gangbangers on the Street and in Prison*. Boulder, CO: Paladin Press, 2000.

Wroblewski, Chris. *Skin Shows: The Tattoo Bible*. London, England: Collins and Brown, 2004.

INDEX

About the Author

Jason Porterfield has written more than twenty books for Rosen Publishing on subjects ranging from American history to environmental science. He earned his undergraduate degree in English, history, and religion from Oberlin College, a school that has not allowed its students to join or form secret societies since the 1930s. While researching this book, he was struck by the long histories of the world's tattooing traditions. He currently lives in Chicago, Illinois.

Photo Credits

Cover © AFP/Getty Images; pp. 5, 23 © Robert Nickelsberg/ Getty Images; p. 7 © Tattoo Archive; p. 8 © The British Library/ HIP/The Image Works; pp. 11, 17, 20 © AP Images; p. 12 Shutterstock.com; p. 18 © Joel Stettenheim/Corbis; pp. 25, 26, 33 © Andrew Lichtenstein/Corbis; p. 29 © David Leeson/ Dallas Morning News/The Images Works; p. 38 © Mary Evans Picture Library/The Image Works; p. 40 © Horace Bristol/ Corbis; p. 43 © Topham/The Image Works; p. 45 © David Turnley/Corbis; p. 48 © Getty Images; p. 52 © Brendan Smialowski/Reportage/Getty Images.

Designer: Les Kanturek; **Editor:** Nicholas Croce
Photo Researcher: Cindy Reiman